Love Letters

Jacob Potash

ISBN: 979-8-9863364-2-8
Price: 9.99 USD
Publication: September 2022
Publisher: Nachlebenone

I.

1. I think I find it hard to tell someone I miss him

And I do, in general, think remarkably little about people I'm not with

But I am imagining sitting together in the morning

2. I feel remote from you. Maybe we're always equidistant.

I like the form of your email and the mind roiling underneath. Though it is not very Foucaultian of me to imagine a mind under the bits of your discourse.

I have been wrestling with this problem for a long time now. I have gone through many epigraphs. I think an epigraph will never mean to somebody else what it means to you. What it means to you should be your book, basically, and that's what is communicable. Or, that is the communication.

You're already full of meaning for me, a harbinger of meaning. I don't want you to be sad, which is (strictly) pathetic.

Sacrifice and severity and separateness seem to be very important to me. Was thinking about this yesterday. I link it to my childhood, when I knew early on that I wouldn't be able to participate in many of the normal pleasures, and so would have to find more difficult pleasures. Or, I was always removed from people, so it wasn't such a burden to continue to keep myself removed.

I can't believe your dad wouldn't speak to you for weeks. Or, I'm troubled by it and don't understand. I like the thought that if you arrange food the right way, something might come through.

I think the epigraph is funny.

One of the applications has to be done today so that's what I'll do.

"Ever,"

3. I just got out of bed
I haven't had coffee. I feel lucky to have been able to crawl out of bed and read your email. Email is a good form. The cognitive music was immense. You're a poet of some kind

Four years ago in Argentina I did not have a computer or smartphone, I had sold them, but I would go to a "kiosk" or shop and pay a few pesos to use a boxy Windows computer, and the only person I communicated with was R I think, and I remember sitting alone in the middle of that stagey city thinking about how a mind can be pressed into an email. Thrilling to words. Thrilling to the music of an email. Feeling love through words.

Dads are problematic. Theme of history is death of fathers. When I lived at home last January I hated it. One day my dad said "Why can't you be more normal" and I flew into a rage.

Thank you for sharing yourself with me, to whatever extent you do. I listened to a lecture about Derrida the other day, did not know anything about him, and heard that a sentence always takes the form of a metaphor, that the predicate "is" never the subject. I am happy. I am sad. I am out of sorts. The plane is flying. I also don't want to ever know anything about postructuralism.

I laughed at "recreationally." I don't think I've had to lie to anyone about a bond of chastity between us. I like the voice messages even better than your emails, probably because you have a nice voice. I also like the pauses and sighs. I wonder what else was said in the conversation with your dad, though I don't like to think of it.

Pardon the desultoriness. There is a little girl who lives across the alley whose voice I can hear. I think the two most beautiful things are trees and children. You are delectable

4. I may write without referring back to your email. Would be an interesting exercise.

I could of course mention my eighth grade girlfriend. I really liked her and it was sort of serious. That made me all the more afraid when I came back from camp at the end of the summer before freshman year. I heard from a friend that she had been hanging out with a popular boy from another school named Avi. I called her and accused her. I can remember her faltering, her tone of embarrassment and confusion. Also, I told her, we're going to different high schools. You're becoming like the vapid BT girls.

I think I'm sorry I've mentioned hooking up. I think it is potentially cruel. I think I'm not sure if I have felt this way, it is irrational and real, literal nausea, I'm being vague now.

Wanting to protect your solitude, your integrity, wanting not to violate some rule of decency, to be restrained and deferential for you, impersonal and reliable—these seem suddenly primary.

5. "Where is Jacob" was so moving to me. Must have to do with the magic power of speech, of names, of houses, of families.

I cried in the movie (and may do so again now) because of the representation of love. In Anna Karenina, around 500 pages in, Levin, the Tolstoy-character, a monk-like rural landowner who's writing a book about agriculture to pass the time, finally proposes to Kitty, I say finally because he endures much in the first 500 pages, and after doing so his older, better-adjusted friend says to him, "Not time to die anymore?"

I listened to somebody read this on a bridge over a river between Queens and Brooklyn at one o'clock in the morning last summer. I talked to my dad about it the next day. He loves me and has helped me at important moments. It was about a year into the writing. How many re-births do we get?

This is no doubt what it's like to be alive. I prefer it. Love is something the troubadours made up a thousand years ago. One mustn't think too hard about it.

"How different things are now, and how similar"!

6. hello sweet masculine
sensitive and reasonable
poetic jewish

levin came to mind because i like him feel a revolution in feeling
a changing-places of the celestial bodies

feelings are forever a personal achievement. i love that you said, i love reading "i want to know more about it. i mean you." dare i say, foolishly and purely, i love you

i had the thought yesterday that our first week is like 'the early church', instantly mythical and irrecoverable

have laughed every time i've read "a medical student at yale university." you're funny. thank you for the metaphor. recuperation. bad into good. i have the prosaic impulse to say something about culture, about cities of the mind, alleys you can wander in. in my last semester i asked my teacher what books i should read for my term paper. he said, "my advice to you is, wander. it's all i've ever done"

i wonder why you were cruel to the boy, yet not really, because there is so much terror then, and i've been cruel too. i look forward to seeing what comes of your life too, i could probably cry at the sentence, it's a strangely passive construction, would never use it for my own life because i do not want to be a beholder, an appreciator of my own existence, and leave it to be lived by someone else.

nietzsche and troubadours - didn't know. be sure of a hot meal and a bed, whitman said. that plays so strongly in me against the rabbis, the ministers who say "the night cometh, when no man can work"

it doesn't matter maybe, if you trust in yourself or don't in yourself. i love motion, speed, novelty (sometimes). i'm imagining you making things. a restaurant, a movie, a sentence. i'm somewhat uncomfortable socially. i wonder if we know each other. we must, though.

7. I don't want you ever to doubt that I feel precisely the same way, even if I can't express it as you do

8. I paused the movie and will start the email. I feel it's my turn.

Here I am on a warm summer night in my apartment. The

movie depresses me with its intellectual foaming. It's like a bad essay. I want to watch Lola with you. It's mythical and classical like a good meal. A dancer, a sailor, a child, a disappointed young man, a crime

When I spoke to my father he disappointed me. At the time I felt relief to talk, wondered how I ever could have directed such rage against him. But now I see I have similar questions to the ones you raise. It's not just that he doesn't know who Antonioni and Kierostami are and could never care to find out. It's that he doesn't wonder about questions of value.

I think in such blunt categories, such abstractions. I think this is a kind of generalized repression. I don't know anything about Freud but the delicate pain, the new subtle pleasures of doing what we're doing is hard for me to keep in the fore.

Did I say this yesterday? I like to think of you as better than me. In a hundred ways. You are having the time of your life. I accepted a while ago that I am too; do I have to remember to say it? Do I begin to know how to say it?

I like your sister

I liked hearing your thinking about the show that Wood wants you to do. Anything to do with business I get so squeamish about. R is good at it, level-headed, I value it in him. You seemed withdrawn on the walk, but I don't need to tease out every thought. I asked if you were happy and believed you and didn't need more.

You are taming me, civilizing me. What i said about the new yorker is a kind of young bullish antagosim that i got too comfortable indulging in the last year. it is lazy to be dismissive of everything.

Someone compares life to a road in which occasionally we hit a rise and gain a view of the road extending into the distance before and behind us.   I never 'dealt' with the waiter: he found me and sent the photographs unsolicited. Enough of that   The Friday night after Frances I had dinner out with P, the last time I've been to a restaurant. I had mentioned the date beforehand but he didn't mention it once the whole night. No problem. Words are infinite and silences are infinite and all of it passes through us. "To the pure, all things are pure."

9. you,

i think you are justified

i lay in bed hungrily awaiting an email last night. i suppose because you told me you had started one. i feel i always need to hear from you, and i do, and it means much to me. it has meaning. strandian meaning

i spent much of the morning going back and forth with R about an idea he has 'in connection with' a short movie he wants to make. i think it's important not to be idle. it's important always to take another step

soon i'll talk to P about his zany mystical hegelian marxist ideas. they bewilder me but i encourage him, for many, many reasons i love that you notice things. i thought when i got in bed that you might notice its state. T said to me once: you don't see physical objects. i think that's changed somewhat. anyway you're better than me

i memorized that sonnet, "trouble deaf heaven with my bootless cries," three or four years ago in my south american isolation, walking down a boulevard in buenos aires that looked almost like los angeles. it made no sense to me, sounded like a foreign language, and besides, i thought, i've never felt this way, will never feel this way, don't want to. now the sonnet sounds like nature itself. truth

i have been thinking what i can call you if i'm monk. i thought of duke. but that's an ugly word. prince i'd be happy with too. baron would be funny no?

it seems very profound what you say about the 'session' yesterday. nothing is more familiar than the fear and the anger that my parents would not notice my feelings, acknowledge my autonomy, would rush me past them toward some goal, would not understand the tragicness of everything. that was how i felt in high school; it might be true (right, perceptive).

what is true: there is no solution to the problem. the feeling is the answer. the name the shape are the art, not a problem to be straightened out. relatedly: i don't like science.

i've begun to think in recent weeks that everything i've ever thought was right. that i should have trusted myself more. that if i didn't like economics, this was something economists should be concerned about. a worthy condemnation. it's all coming into view...

i am wondering whether your reflections on your parents are... how much they would occupy you if you were elsewhere. whether the piquancy of them is a function of your being around them.

new air is very pretty. i feel the same. that it is not a feeling i am entering but a whole country, with new customs and intractable problems and so forth. i am very glad to have broken through. to have discovered the new world

i am speaking to you in a particular way, in my own whimsical language, it's very trusting i guess, and you're doing the same i think.

your dad, he hasn't been punitive has he? i knew someone once whose mom read his texts when he was 16 and informed him he wasn't gay. simple!

a teacher, i only sat in on one class, but he said: the words don't matter in this poem

i could cry typing that for some reason. it is remarkable to think: what i feel, what i know, is somehow the result of everything i've ever tasted, seen, thought. wendy williams and south africa and tolstoy and depression and on to infinity. (I laughed at "Don't kill me.") The point being: i think this might be the point of religion, of education, of the best things: to know a good thing when you see it: to know what will sustain you and save you. to know what you can live without.

nothing is better than being beside you. i am having truly perverted thoughts. fuck. talk soon

10. "I think I see it that way because it is real." It's very brave to accept the real. I think dua lipa says in that song, "I could say yes in real life."

I'm moved by the idea that I will understand your simplicity and you'll understand mine. This seems sacred. It is not simple to be simple. It is and it isn't.

I believe that conclusions are the best way to begin, if you can learn to hear them the right way.

"Speaking, as writing, is a mnemonic (pneumonic) device." Yes, a simple yes. Speech is magic, practically. I guess that's as much as to say, the relationships between it and memory and meaning are too complex to analyze, and always getting more complex, more elusive.

(Language is a dirty projector)

I have felt (known?) for a long time that (I guess you agree) there is nothing that can't be confronted, nothing you can't be honest about. The more you absorb, the more you are capable of absorbing. Everything feels light, lighter given that you said what you said. It foreshortens the imagination, to tell the truth. Imagination is irreponsible, unfriendly.

For a while I felt my relationships with P and T were the two most intense of my life, or the two "best friends" I had ever had. R probably superseded that in the time since college ended. My two years with them started in fear and disgust, and ended in a deep awareness of their limitations, their blindnesses, their emotional gaps and stuntings; there is pathos in that because in between was so much closeness, so much love, admiration. Trauma probably too.

I think the symmetry is elegant. I think it is a nice certification of reality, that we know the same people. I think it makes perfect, earnest sense—that everyone is worthy and deserving, you know, and that young men are drawn to each other for good reasons.

fascinating that you say the name became a shorthand. i have been thinking just in the last week about how certain names and faces become symbols, demons, inhuman, shorthands in the unconscious. i read yesterday that the psalms try to make gratitude into a mode of cognition. i don't know if i am capable of that; but maybe i have an investigation to mount. This is what i tried to write a letter to you about the other day.

every second,

11. Writing this email on my phone, I could keep this volley going day after day

Presently. Main-tenant. Holding in hand
English, French, Latin

It has become a shorthand for what I have found in you: there is poetry in that: the interchangeability of names. T means Jacob. Why not

What a wonderful slip, or contraction, or symbol: "as." Like or as. The space between was and is

You're right to push gently further, I did not quite say anything. T is a friend for life, a brother, though we go many months without speaking. In January or February we had dinner and he slept at my apartment. We speak in a very impersonal way. For a while I thought the drugs had ruined his mind forever, now I'm not sure. We have spent many hours discussing what friendship is

I remember saying to S that it had been nice, in New York, to be reacquainted with friends from childhood I hadn't seen in six or seven years; I was struck when he sneered and said he wasn't in touch with anybody he grew up with. As if to do so would be provincial.

Here is another sonnet, with an uncanny music:

Were't aught to me I bore the canopy,
With my extern the outward honouring,
Or laid great bases for eternity,
Which prove more short than waste or ruining?
Have I not seen dwellers on form and favour
Lose all, and more, by paying too much rent,
For compound sweet forgoing simple savour,
Pitiful thrivers, in their gazing spent?
No, let me be obsequious in thy heart,
And take thou my oblation, poor but free,
Which is not mix'd with seconds, knows no art
But mutual render, only me for thee.
Hence, thou suborn'd informer! a true soul

When most impeach'd stands least in thy control.

Bloom would ask us what was meant by "pitiful thrivers." No one could say.

You seem to me the opposite of miniature coked and afraid of stopping. You are large and thoughtful. I am enamored of etymologies, and marvel at the primal meanings of words. "Research" means "circus" which means "circle," roughly. One can only argue about ideas using symbols that mean: circle, bend, jump, pointy, do.

12. P said that we don't need to plan, and that I don't need to explain myself to you. I said you're right

It makes me happy to hear about the numerology etc. I think I know what you wish to communicate. Why does melancholia come to mind? Or why does unfinished business come to mind?

Doesn't it take confidence to be fragile?

I want you always to respond about everything. Maybe this is selfish, my bias. I remember telling R in one of the first weeks of freshman year that I wouldn't wish childhood on my worst enemy.

I'm glad you feel bitterness is a sin. I'm glad of you. I think much of my adolescence I spent sympathizing with women; sometime later I must have sided with men, realized that too much sympathy would kill me.

13. used to have a dream when I was young did I tell you this?

The dream. The dream as I can remember it is that I am running or skipping through a house with a boy my age, it's a big house in some secluded place, there are other people it's nighttime it may be a big family gathering, but we're upstairs and skipping past rooms with people in them and go into a secluded room with red velvet and slanted ceilings and soft light and ledges and mirrors and it's almost like a closet and we sit on the ledges maybe in each other's laps and swing our legs and kiss and it's our secret and we are boys and playmates and trust each other and have perfect privacy, intimacy, I had this when I was 11 or 12 or 13 and when I would try to tell myself I wasn't gay I would remember that dream and hope, complexly.

Yes, the dream is like a dream of swimming. We run down the hallway and into the room with a certain fluidity, our bodies are like in a painting, not solid or clumsy or separate.

I wonder if I have expressed myself. I think I have. In the last seven or eight months I learned to see sex in a new way—as like fiction-writing, as vapid as that sounds. I want to produce and experience every effect. I like experimentation. I like manipulating myself, seeing my body or yours as puppets, materials for art. Think of it: one day we could really do anything together, and it wouldn't mean anything, anything ultimate, wouldn't express our essences, it would just be for itself, and that's why it would be perfect.

14. I am tempted into saying, or rather I noticed, that may-

be I know why your dad gets "mad." I mean that it was hard for me, I was uneasy, reading about the door closing on your head, and whatever "scene" that must have entailed. Maybe he gets mad at you because he loves you. Maybe there are other more salient reasons. Maybe he knows things I or you don't know.

I am realizing I misread part of your email. That I thought you said you were trying to imagine men as other than versions of their father. That would have made less sense. I am tempted to ask more about ****'s behavior—whether you'd say he has a temper; whether he is "proud," or emotionally vulnerable. You, needless to say, have never made me mad.

The related point that I have wanted for some time to broach, which now might be a good time to bring up, is that given how I work, given my temperament or spurts of determination, I can say there will likely be times when I need to be without distractions or to be especially isolated, for days, maybe more. This is not impending; I have only wanted to mention it since you raised that anxiety. (I think at the time I hadn't even noticed that I'd been quiet or taken longer than usual in responding.)

Now I remember your message (I get chills) about the lake and the forest and the adjoining rooms. And what you said about me on a bed behind you reading a book with a colon in the title. And I think, that would be living; that what I am doing now might be something less.

I thought after our walk yesterday that I should be cautious not to yield to the... temptation? (that is not a term I think in), to the mindless habit, rather, of thinking you are a second me, of lazily treating you as an extension of myself. It is fortunate even to have this problem, this almost-possibility. But I found myself less than alive to you... there is a tension between giving in to the warmth of knowing you and retaining a sense of wonder at your otherness... a respect for the sense in which I don't know you...

I am fond of pistachio ice cream...

Oh. I meant to get to something else. I've noticed the refrain in your letters—it sounds for all the world as if you are saying it to yourself, trying to work yourself up to it—that you should leave your parents' house, that the time has come. I like hearing you say it. It is both very direct, and indirect.

It is funny that I only meant to stay here a month or two. It is funny that I am now 'engaged' to stay in this place at least till the end of June, likely longer. It is funny that, even though I have told my mom I'll be doing a Greek course in June and July, I may not; I haven't decided. I mean to ask her about whether and when it will be possible to visit the lake (New Hampshire). It's funny that... I'd go anywhere in the world with you.

Remember when I asked you to live with me? I barely do; how long ago was it? How reasonable or unreasonable? I suppose I'm asking you again now, or at least opening that door a little wider. I was thinking after June I might switch to someplace cheaper. Isn't anywhere cheaper than here...? (Cole has upped the price & I'm spending slightly beyond my means.)

Remember when you sprawled on my couch and said "if we

were to live together… hypothetically"? I should admit that the idea scares me, since I prize freedom and have never lived with someone in this way. It would be what they call a first.

15. I am sitting alone on my couch and suddenly it seems hard

I am imitating your style I guess. I think I like to imitate people's styles
Sometimes I find myself imitating your cadences
The way you say hello
I used to think it's because I didn't know who I am.
But being like someone else changes who you are
Can't let these lines get too long

Today was extremely hot. Are we getting better
and better?

I think about right now, and the future, and the last year, and think
I am not good at just living. I like to be transitioning
To something new. I like extremes.
I want to get better at living.

When I stopped being friends with those girls
(They were respected, popular, had important 'positions' on 'campus')
I stopped being part of a 'scene.' I moved into the house.
I didn't want to assimilate myself to a scene, wanted
To forge something thoroughgoing and individual
With a few friends.

I did that with R too and I am doing it with you

And I didn't turn my back on everything:
R N G P - these were the friends I made the first
week of college. It's nice to rememeber that there are those
Who know me. (We have been efficient
in getting to know each other.)

I don't know how to tell you how it makes me feel
To hear you say my letter made you cry.

I love the image of the grill, the coals, learning to clean it
learning to find wood, heat it properly. What you say
About painting, about me, about walking.
It can be difficult to start. The summer after graduation I was in
New Haven and would go to a field to record
Sort of diary entries, into a recorder. Hard to say why
And when I would walk and speak a kind of magic would happen,
I could learn amazing things, take flights of fancy
But when it wasn't happening I couldn't believe it
And had to renew my faith each morning

You are different than me. You seem better than me at living, which
is wrong to say, in a few senses, but there it is:
I guess the simplest thing to say is
I am amazed by your cooking, and painting
And the emails are like compositions, layered, simmered, etc.

I just noticed Google's suggestion that I 'add' this email to 'Tasks'
I wont. It is not

"Learn to give each other peace when he needs"
Just makes me want to cry, or exhale quickly, or deeply

"I think we could create something that suits us"
Some things bear repeating, 'publishing'. I publish
Your words to you. What I said about people saying
Am I making any sense? after saying what makes the most sense:
My favorite part was your saying what foods you do not like to eat and why
And that you would eat rice and beans for every meal
Me too
Me too
Me too

I want to risk living with you.

This is all funny
and actual and devastating, but the only alternative is
numbness, passiveness, having your life lived for you
By forces outside of yourself.

I just mean I am scared too. Walking down the street
Arms around each other feels good. Simple? simple?
I worry that partnerships of this kind are a kind of bad religion
- Not that they have to be, but that with no authority,
No text, no power to hold to, people expect salvation from their
(I'll use the word) boyfriend, or something.
I think value is outside of us, and inside of us, but

we are not responsible for the other's happiness, in
an ultimate sense

(Gay is a bizarre euphemism, was already outdated
eighty years ago)

Just a life together - is poignant. That's all, no pressure,
just a life together. A town in northern california - sounds -
what could be better? I have a tiny "income." Maybe could
work on the side
Would have to live very cheaply
And so forth

This is very new for me. I have never really done this before.
I have spent a long time avoiding something like this.
Because I knew if it happened, if I decided for it to happen
I would be... trustworthy. Strange as it is to insist on it: I am
trustworthy.
Not the most creative or intuitive or normal boyfriend
But trustworthy

I guess I should say both that I felt distant
from you at some moments today and that that is to be expected,
That I am verbal and needy in my way, and too cheerful and
don't know
How to sanctify a moment (how to be restrained). I wonder
if you
felt uneasy not having heard from me, after... having taken
a risk.

I'm very sleepy. I don't want to proofread this. I just want to talk to you

In one way,

16. Here I was thinking I'd have to go to bed disgruntled, inarticulate
Watching the matrix left me disgruntled
Why? I think the language of sermons and the
Language of the bible and the thought of all
The history they have led to seem more
Imaginative and more like magic and that
The movie was reaching for something it couldnt get

I like that when you're reading a book you're just reading a book

Or that when you're lying on a couch with someone you're really lying on a couch with him

Not looking at a woman in black latex with a nose job do stunts with cgi from 1999

I don't know. I'm glad I have the image of last night in my head forever. Maybe i tell you how
You are too often
But you are so
Delicate is wrong, magnetic is wrong, alive is wrong
But they're also right, when you moved to sit next
To me and when you said the thing about answering
My questions and feeling on edge and I got to look at you

I don't need much. I think I've proven that to myself this last while. (Is that true? Can that be true?) Or - only a few things of a high quality.

I'm remembering the email when you started enumerating the minimum of what you could live with
That moved me. That impulse moved me
I think trying to live on as little as possible
Was something that started when I thought I wanted just to write, to do as little else as possible
But that is changing, has been changing. I want to be part of something I think, do more for others

I'm going back to thinking about watching you sitting next to me
What do I want to say - just that that happened
On May 29
Just that, if nothing else, may 29 was a significant day

I'm remembering the second time I saw Harold bloom he was in a bad mood (he was very sick) and liked my paper less than the first time, and said "well, now I've read your paper twice"
He loved to be accurate
Historical
To mark times passage and its effects on him
An artistic impulse
(To complain)
That also reminds me that I worry
That when I'm in class or in school again
I'll be very busy
Won't be able to make you feel like you've heard from me
Often enough
As you'd like

17. I woke up, read your email, went to sleep, woke up, reread it, slept. So it
has been passed through my unconscious mind. Sifted through sleep
Was the object of reveries

That was hours ago now. I have since then thought of so many things to say
There are many things I find myself wanting to say to you over and over
I wonder if I know what it's like for you to live in your house - I don't really
Or if you know what it's like for me to be here alone - not really
I thought of how happy I'd be to hug R or to hug my mom
Even though I know it wouldn't be exactly reciprocated
If only because nothing is exactly reciprocated

That wasn't how I wanted to start. Let's see
A psalm says "Stand in awe, and sin not.
Commune with your own heart upon your bed, and be still."
Isn't that something? I swear I am not becoming a fanatic. I think I just have interests, find new interests, exactly as you predicted I would.
My parents would remark on the fact that I went through phases
Extremely intense
Painting was one. Maybe the violin was one. Cars, when I was in third grade
My campaign to save Darfur - have we discussed that?

We are beings in time, to be sure. I reflexively, given my interest, want to say, are we also beings in god? One of Marilynne's most
astonishing sentences comes to mind: something like: the prohibition on
teleology must be arbitrary, given that we don't yet know what time is.
She stands in awe

I guess I very emphatically agree: that I, too, want what I want
eat what i want, and give up on wanting when the whole vision
is not my own. That's a very beautiful formulation on your part
I think of it as related to depression, which is a psychiatric term.
I think I just have high standards. I think LA was part of my whole vision.
I always used to think: I'd like to live somewhere beautiful.
I'm looking out my window now at a tree, red stucco, white lining, empty sky all fully illuminated

I guess I want to say: maybe an answer to what do we want from each other
is company, to keep company. It is my dream, what you said, roughly -
to know to leave each other alone, to need you as a witness and
nothing more, strictly speaking. I'm speaking now (content and style)
in a way I've never spoken before. We've talked about this, though

In a strange way we've talked about everything already

That family friend David takacs ended the email, "Congratulations, by the way,
on having chosen to be born into a great and loving family."
Which is right and wrong,
Funny and serious. I'm sure the way my dad talks about me surprised him,
or moved him. So I say to you, congratulations. I remain interested
in why you are ashamed, what the castigation was over, whether you'd feel
differently if you were away from them. Does it go without saying that
I feel for you, I know the feeling, and I don't know the feeling? That I don't
want you to feel ashamed, that you have nothing to be ashamed for?

Everything you say about being a child is...
subtle. I was a bad child too, I got in trouble
often for arguing with teachers. I've always sought for a teacher I could respect.

Milton was obsessed with digestion, with constipation, with farting, the relationship
Of food to the body, the mind, speech, prayer, God, poetry.
Of how to make everything integral with everything else. Of how to make
everything usable, nothing evil.

I love the way your body feels against my arm around your back...

The organizing principle of reality is complexity, but we can decide to be simple
I will brush harder, more often

I meant to say: I rode on the wave of your thoughts.
I love getting a very long message
from you because I know I'll be held aloft by it

I meant to say: I wonder if I know less or more now
Than I did two months ago

I meant to say: this is a space of freedom
Writing is a space of freedom
The soul is a space of freedom
Friendship is a space of freedom

Strangely I feel more genuinely
Engaged in life than ever. When I came back to school
I was at Elena's apartment with others, standing in the doorway
To the living room, and Pablo said come in, play cards with us,
And I said no, I'm... outside of it. And he said, no Jacob, you're in it
You're in it

You must be right. Suffering is good because it is necessary. That's a complicated
Claim to make. Jesus says, the poor you will always have with you, but me you
do not have always. Isn't that hilarious? There is no truth, only a complex order,

a simple uninterpretable pattern, a hand on the back, air off a golf course.

ps I don't think you are autistic

ps
I wonder what it would mean
To see your family as if for the first time
Or yourself

18. i am shuddering still

i am very tired

the book revived me

you seem capable of reminding me what matters. i feel now somewhat as i did when i finished death in venice. (march thirteenth?) i read each too fast, the way books should be read

(i'm courting you)

(a certain clarity emerges in disruption. when i came here, for example. or when you met me?)

(the most useful principal for criticism i have ever come across is by oscar wilde: it is something like: the only proper attitude toward art is receptiveness)

I wrote down a few sentences as I read but in light of the final chapters they seem inadequate. I do hear your voice, at moments. I think I have to say that I like the final chapter least. Something is lost when the secret is told outright. I also reflected, maybe for the first time, that I suppose I do feel a certain disgust at an open description of homosexuality. I am receptive to that feeling.

(What is literature?)

I will end on this abrasive note

19.
Marilynne Robinson is a griffith, a torso,
an illustration in the sky
above Los Angeles, her body spelled
and spelling, Maintenance and Reproduction
In two letters and three arches:
MR.

It is dusk. Poetry is a mnemonic.
Headlights dim down the mountain.
Tomorrow I will sign up for
A babysitting website.

20. Dear —,
I just cried listening to a podcast about Harold Bloom that included recordings of his interview on the radio program. I have (had two beers?) often reflected that Harold Bloom must have been the love of my life. In Iowa I discovered him, at 15 or 16, going to the library downtown before I'd made any friends.

He was concerned with ultimate things. That is finally the distinction that matters. He reveled in the grand impersonality of the general... his theory of literary history was one of original strength and subsequent decline (belatedness), and that scheme had the benefit of making literary criticism the only genre with the potential to join the highest rank of—

I will turn toward the particular. I think I could be a very good academic but that the whole institution is too compromised; that you as a faculty member or aspirant are too beholden to others, and that scientific, social-scientific, or other dogmas have penetrated too deeply to be sidestepped or overcome within a university department. These are matters I have had ricocheting in my skull for years and it is hard to crystallize them, to know how to formulate them. My point is that I want to be a writer. Yes...

What am I saying? That I need you to come with me? That I looked at you on the trail today and couldn't believe you were real? I enjoy so much being close to you that I don't have many opportunities to stand back & admire you; enjoy touching you so much that I can't enjoy the restrained pleasures of distance—those difficult pleasures...

People are so mediocre and middling and boring and unfree. What am I saying! What am I saying! I am talking about my life, my sense of what I am called to do, my sense of what is important. I don't think I am smart, but there are exuberances in me that need to be realized and indulged.

21. i think it's my duty to say I am not always quite so optimistic. I have struggled for long periods with... "feeling down."

22. Dear —,

(Do I mean that? Will I show you this? It's late; I'm drinking; it's always late) When I take walks without my phone mental gels, mists, bursts descend... hazes, tints, splashes, darknesses, constellations, temples. A great unmixed masterpiece seems to accrue as i walk; consciousness in the absence of other wills (oh no - here I go) seems to flower, bloom, unfold in the duskiest most gorgeous most sublime way. Dear —! — —.

I like to, I try to always, absorb facts into some great generalization, fold them into some important pattern, which is one reason I suspect I'd never make a really good artist in any medium. I'm impatient for the truth (always), and art is something other than the truth. Art requires patience. Art is what comes when you wait for it.

And now I am thinking of you swimming, or you driving, or me getting into the passenger's seat for the first time, or my laying my head on your lap in Beverly Hills or on the bench overlooking the city just down from the observatory. I marveled today at the timing of all this... I at least, after a few idle and confused months, was suddenly ready; and you in some sense were too... why not make recourse to religious language? It was fate? It can't be wrong, it can't be untrue, to say this. It can only be meaningful.

23. "When I said you were strange, I meant objectively"

Dear —,

I just, while I was eating brown-rice fusili, watched an Adam Phillips interview and, noticing the bizarre music halfway through, realized it must be the one you told me about.

(Your writing sounds the way your paintings look!)

("It was the exemplary that I wanted to know and understand"!)

Who gave you permission to write a gorgeous essay about... your profound experience of a teacher (the erotics of pedagogy) and the nature of criticism! Much less to get it published.

I hope and expect quite confidently that I'll never forget "the world has immediacy. this immediacy is its meaning." Writing it that way, lower-case, makes it look almost like modernist poetry, which reminds me that Adam Phillips gives wonderful book recommendations in that interview. The meaning of the last month surely was its immediacy. No criticism of it is possible, least of all by me, because I have not stopped to think, I have merely stayed in perpetual motion. I thought I had been acting instinctually, but it turns out I have been acting "immediately." Though maybe there is no other way to act—no other mediation than consciousness or memory, no matter how long we wait for it. We are always ourselves, alone, immediately...

(I read about Martin Luther this morning.)

Do you want to try living in New York this summer? Together? I decided (somehow) today to sign up for the Colorado Boulder class, somewhat less intensive than the others, because life is too important to be taken seriously, and it is not good to study too hard. Augustine was the greatest of Christian Platonists, and he never read Plato. You see what I mean? Would your parents let you stay in the apartment? Would they require you to find a job fast? Would they charge you rent? Because if they didn't I could cover everything else. Would they be averse to your taking a class? (I wouldn't need to make a final decision about next year till sometime in the middle of summer.)

A glass of red aided in the composition of this; I repent nothing. It is forceful and to the point; or not. I'll send it in the morning, because otherwise I won't sleep.

Humbly yours,

24. It's morning. I'm drinking coffee. Looking back at "domestic and masculine at once."

You are someone I've dreamt of for many years.

I like looking at you equally from different distances — 20 feet, 10, 5, .1.

Maybe I'll stay in this room over the summer. Maybe we should wait to go any further. I could imagine living here next year, too. Could you imagine living in London? Is there art in London?

I can't believe I am a muse. I like the idea.

Postscript. I am moved by your saying "in friendship, and more." You are so complete.

More postscript. It is after noon now. Reread your letter: you don't speak too much! I wish you would speak even more. I very much prefer listening to speaking. I have the same anxiety.

25. I've been meaning to read the Book of Daniel — the prophet Daniel — I hear it's dark and strange.

It's early evening (I'm having a beer before dinner — it's nice to deprive yourself arbitrarily, to not have beer for a few weeks, or apples — variety itself...), but nearly time to go to bed. I will go to sleep not long after it gets dark and rise just before it gets light.

I watched an interview between the televangelist Pat Robertson and Donald J. Trump from October 2016 today; both are worth hundreds of millions of dollars, are religious figures, politicians, created semi-fake universities, build buildings, host television shows. Trump comes off wonderfully in it. They both seem wonderfully intelligent, earnest, playing their parts well, poised... there is an earnestness in the right kind of lie, if it's suitably grand and purposeful. They seem to me very American, such men, such lies,

Evangelicals like to talk about keeping Jesus at the head of their marriage. This too seems wise. It's something like what I meant the other day about the 'bad religion' of 'relationships'. Marriage is a formal and civilized and practical convention; our knowledge of other people is partial; and the ideal, the ritual a relationship comprises, must be realized or carried out with reference to civilizational canons... to God... to a community, to anything but the other person. Sorry for speaking this way. It is impulsive and not carefully elaborated.

If I do the Greek for the next two months, we will have considerably less time to spend together. Granted, it's temporary. Also, if we lived in the same place it would be—well, easier to see each other. Maybe in June we can spend the weekends together. Maybe we will begin to be able to have meals. I am not yet sure what the right 'course' is. I would be lonely here all week. I see dogs and children at the park and find corresponding... stirrings in me.

I must sound different here—in ink, on paper—

26. maybe my anxiety, or my demon, is to wonder if people are telling the truth, to see layers of motivation and tactical brilliance beneath every utterance

has to do with my saying I think everyone is a genius
and my asking the question about your mom that you hated

you are in the best way, simple

it's so obvious to me in this moment

feels almost depraved to have second guessed it, speculated maliciously about it

forgive me. your original message was so lovely, concise, straightforward

as always

27. Subject line: "On What You Might Do With Your Life."

    I'm always starting letters to you then getting embarrassed or... rhapsodic. I intend to show you this one. Or all the other ones, eventually.

    Emerson when he was 24, with a respiratory problem, left Boston for the beach somewhere in Florida, where he met Napoleon's nephew (also named Napoleon), with whom he took long walks and who became a lifelong friend.

    Joyce absconded with his Catholic barmaid to the French Riviera and taught piano lessons in genteel poverty while writing Ulysses.

    Borges lived in an apartment with his mother for his whole life. Pynchon went to the west coast and lived in a cottage. Ashbery, to France, to write about art.

    I've been reading obituaries. "Doctor." "Lawyer." "Scholar." That's what I mean about plans and stereotypes—

these peoples' obituaries are prewritten when they're 24. I read a biography of Borges once. When he was 60, he became very famous. Of course he had been writing for 30 years. It was around age 40 that he found his voice. This is the real drama of his life and an audience can accrue to it only long after the fact.

28. i want to make a monument to the walk i just took, give testimony of it, although to do so feels like trying to capture a sandstorm in a plastic container.

  Last January when I stayed home, one day my grandmother came from Pennsylvania for lunch with her retinue, two ladies in waiting, women who'd been devoted to her for years. She wore a navy blazer with gold buttons and a plain pink shirt under it and she looked magnificent, casually feminine, breezily regal... I loved her but respected her too much, feared her; and didn't know how to speak with her. I said something about what I'd be doing—she misheard; perked up and looked pleased—said, "You're doing finance?" And I hated to have to say no—Brooklyn, writing, teaching, whatever. After she died I considered that I must have been an embarrassment to her, and how gracious she was with me, considering: gay and Jewish. She would have liked me to row crew and work on Wall Street.

  P has little wisdom but despite himself, intuitively, he understands much, and once he said, "Adults love to give you unsolicited advice, and the secret is, you should never take it." I think about Greek, about finance, about the University of Wisconsin Madison, which a teacher said should be my top choice.

  Plenty of smart things have been said about the significance of silences. On a tour in Greece, the woman said, "What the men cared about most they never spoke of." I've had trouble till now picturing you when I'm not with you. This, its own psychological ellipsis. Its own silence, repression, covering. But today halfway up the mountain a vision came to me of you looking over and smiling at me; I came to a clearing overlooking the city at dusk, in haze, and saw the smile hovering in the sky like a dove on the abyss or like Marilynne Robinson. I wondered later if love is idolatry, impiety, but no, love is the whole of the law, or else love is madness, and madness is beyond religion altogether.

What was I saying?

Words. Newspapers. Literary magazines. Tweets. Novels. Philosophy. I like the notion that a certain kind of young man devotes himself to words so as to hedge round a great silence; so as to guard his secret in a fortress of civilized speech, repressed insignificance.

Sometimes I feel I could write forever. There is a great debate running through literature and philosophy between dualism and monism. But even to use such terms is already to commit yourself to a kind of silly fixity, a dualism, a sundering. I just want to say whatever comes to mind. The thought came to mind today that you are my witness: are proof that I exist. Merci.

PS I sent the first two pages and thought "I wonder what time it is where he is." Then I thought of my sixteenth birthday, and eighteenth, all drops in the puddle of time; remembered it has always been the same time for you as for me; an ironclad law; you don't have to explain anything.

(Time and chronology and tradition and memory and identity are all erased and recreated and transfigured in... really good moments. A good author reverses time, reconfigures the past in an arbitrary, capricious way. That's what you've done, or I've done, or something.)

29. Jealousy is very common and very painful but not exactly real. I had a moment of light and lightness, sort of the turning of a key, coming down the hill today wherein I understood that we all ought to accept each other; that we are drawn to people for good reasons and must coexist. That is the important thing.

When I told you I was sad the other day it was because I "decided" that I couldn't move forward with the novel because of what it said about my experience of romantic attraction. But it was fleeting and years ago, for one thing, and I don't know how you might tend to react to this kind of thing for another, and finally, it's art.

And yet — I won't do it if it would hurt you.

I am strangely blunt, no?

30. Hello, Hello sweetheart,

Can I call you that? I think it is time for another letter. A man outside my window is saying "bird poop," "creamy stuff," "wax." He is fixing a car. The sky is still soft blue white but I suspect it is almost 8. I'll know by the slow rattles and cheers.

I have faith in you, is one thing I thought to say.

I got a long email from an old friend that made me happy. It reminded me how strange my condition has been. Alone with a few books and internet. In a way to be able to survive like that was my dream. But if it's fulfilled that just means I can begin the real work... my real work.

I have no clue how to frame, think of, conceive of the last two months. What springs to mind: magic, miracles, fate. (Just took a sip of Hérètique.) How can there have been time for it all? Astonishing things you have written to me in emails occur to me, and they seem outside of time. What's strange about life is that it contains so many infinities. How can you fit so many infinities in one place?

I think it is important not to sleep some nights, to be on edge some mornings, emotional some afternoons. I don't feel I will be ready, fully mature, for many years. I think of myself as still in training (still soft and bluewhite), and I think you can understand that.

Was just thinking I lost something large and irrecoverable when Bloom died. That that wound was very large and will probably always remain. I want to say something about what love is... what people are... what we can know of them...

I want to see your drawings and paintings in person, I am realizing—I want to hear how you began to draw, why, what it was like. I am imagining your telling me in a voice note, lying on your bed.

31. i just talked to zack
the call had funny contours, characteristic - took its usual turns
but at the end i asked, point-blank i think is the right adverb, what i should do
where i should go
and he synthesized things wonderfully
was a friend
reminded me how happy i've been here
described returning home as a regression of sorts

said he selfishly wants me to be around
and many things besides
encouraged me to think on the order of weeks, and no further

i think it's hard to convey how wrapping, swaddling, warm, lively, life-giving
being with your family over the weekend was for me (maybe this sounds funny)
not only because i have been alone so often and so far from family
but because there are no nuclear families left in my immediate circle:
you seemed offended when i said rob's family was normal, and that normalcy was refreshing
but i think your family, too, is gorgeously normal.
a backyard, challah, wine, a grandmother and her counterpart, a rented car
choosing worn shirts from a suitcase, lying on the bed, waiting for you
to come out of the bathroom

surely by now i have mentioned that borges wrote an essay
set out to prove that time did not exist
did not think of this as fiction, or even irony
wanted to write good philosophy
it has been largely ignored (it lacks a sense of humor)

my eye is changing
somehow you have helped me to make more generous assumptions about people
surely it is because in some sense i have more to give

"i feel i am just beginning to understand it"

me too

somehow, somehow, (no one knows how) it moves me immensely to see you say
there is something in history worth mining
the idea that all art is contemporary when it is before you: is an amazing one.
i listened to prufrock this morning and it was perfectly contemporary
it spoke with a human voice, like yours

i confess i'm overwhelmed by the paragraph about your conscientious and self-preserving ways
i've had my share of losing my will in that of another. it's followed by a retraction of my will into
itself, i think, typically, which is a process that allows for, or generates, or is definitive of, meaning.
talking to you, writing to you, is a meditation,
helps me understand who i am and what i want.
as for telling you what i want: being forthright: and so forth
i suppose it is to live in a civilized and affectionate way
which seems easier with you than without you

i wonder if i have ever loved you more than i do right now or less?
it seems like a relation, a condition, that is given, stable, simple

ps. i am grateful too, it is very sweet for you to say

pps. could it be possible that we started emailing in late april

32. It can't be a bad idea to jot down what I'm thinking

I am going back to school because I want... a new set of words, a new infancy, total humility

I wonder if my posting that picture rattled you

(I am just as confused by your not realizing that we have trouble talking, as by our trouble talking. On walks it was possible — in messages written or spoken, possible. But when we lay on my couch after sex, or had our first meals, we? you? never seemed to... let words flow. Words have their tragic inadequacy; but they are how I relate to people)

I am going home on Saturday, as I suggested.

You spoke eloquently yesterday as always. You said you didn't feel I was speaking to you or to your unhappiness... my first months here I felt energized or inspired, that I always knew what to do, that my footing was sure. I feared no longer feeling this way. And I now no longer feel this way. That is why I wanted a change of scenery: New York, the Bay, Encinitas. I suppose I... want to be held: I don't feel very good, and want to be loved despite that (like a baby!). As you said yesterday: too much responsibility. As you said before: it's all anyone wants.

33. i trust you, you've done nothing to give me any reason to feel less than trusting and respectful toward you and happy that we met

i don't want you to be sad. i am more than hurt, but still I want everything good for you

i am here too
i am struggling with the ugliness of my response
i will always be happy to hear you, to try to see you (beautiful challenge)

34. The only way I have learned to live, to bear living, to find my footing, is to accept a fiction, to fit my circumstances into the shape of a story - and then to lose myself in the rush of living it out, bringing off the intended effect. A relationship is a story, raising children is a story, sin and redemption and apocalypse is a story. In the spring I decided you were a convincing protagonist... I cast you; I committed to you; I took one of the great risks of my life, and emotional worlds, realities and pains, opened to me that wouldn't have existed to me had I not entertained faith in a mirage, or in contingent pleasures, shimmering experiences. If I knew more about Heidegger I could talk about what you have meant to me in his language. But I know "thrownness" - "finitude" - "care" - "time." Making a decision requires conjuring up as much information, as many relevant considerations, as possible; summoning the right constellation of memory (this is why politics is so fraught: behind all values, all normativity, all action, is the mystery of one mind... making up its mind); at the center of the swarm there has to be will, desire, an interested party. To land on a specific object, a certain person, must be a matter of culture, or convention. But I long ago (the year 0) decided that I want you, and to contradict this decision would incur considerable discontinuity. Whatever the stakes of the

story of my life - those, I guess, are the stakes of losing you.

When I said "irrespective of past present and future" I meant - whatever happens.

Whatever happens, something extraordinary has been allowed to bloom. Something... beautiful, honest, human, immediate. Something merely itself.

And despite it all, I wasn't happy living at your house. And despite it all, we were born into different corners of the universe, and we seem both somewhat annoyed at the other's corner.

Two men can do anything they want, and we are free to be queer, which is to say free. Free to shape our ends. "Free artists of ourselves." I mean let's not play with concepts or norms. If I got a PhD and saw you in five years, I would want to embrace you. Let's speak our minds, and be more alive than we're expected to be.

And and and and: you are still a mystery. In your simultaneous sensitivity—about digestion, or cleanliness, or openness to the gentlest thoughts (the baby's first season is also its fourth)—and cruelty, or at least bro-iness, or at least insensitivity—your willingness to insult your mom or—or me (telling me I look like an ugly cartoon character). I value the latter, and maybe I'm that way too, and I'm usually able to laugh with you, but I struggle with thinking about how these spirits mix in you.

35. I am in the airport, listening to tight connection and

thinking of the couch, the bed, the car, crying under my mask and hat and hand

I know there must be a way for me to express that I have sympathy for you

A way for me to not take all of it defensively, a way for me to take you at your word

I'm sorry that I'm just learning now
I'm sorry I didn't master it (art of sadness)

You hold a piece of me still and having it tampered with
Is not a pain that I can make sense of yet
Without gnashing, biting, losing control

I'm sorry

36. I'm on a flight
Another trope -

I have to hold two thoughts

The first is that I knew you needed too much from me (were upset when I said I had work to do or didn't respond to an email till the morning)—knew I would not be able to write that way or complete my studies that way—knew that I had little interest in painting or you in religion—knew that I did not want to watch sitcoms together—knew that I was too young to be a spouse.

But I also had an idea about love
It was fed in April when you wrote a poem
In French that imagined I was your husband
It was fed in May by the sculpture that
said, I love you. It was fed by the email
of two weeks ago that said, I love you more
than I have ever loved anybody. It was fed
on Sunday when you said, I've decided: a
week here and two in San Diego. It was an
idea about a love that was not defeated by
a week of frustration, or by "horniness," and
one that lasted more than a season.

I thought several times in the last few
weeks about what you have called
your snapchat romances, the relationships
that lasted a summer, before frustration
set in. I thought: spring has passed,
the snap has expired, he has done
this enough times.

I am not sure you had any responsibility
to me. For example, to give me more
than two days' notice that I wouldn't
have a home or a partner anymore. Or,
to raise the concerns that were the source
of the frustration in June.

In any case I hope you can understand why I can't be sure of
the kind things you say now. My
first instinct is to believe you, to feel I
know you; the second is to cynically
recognize the trope, it's not you it's me,

to remember that you've done this before,
and cringe with self-pity. Even I feel
that these words are unfair to you. But
the sweet words feel unfair, or at best
empty, when paired with what is happening.

Maybe I should have tried to speak
more clearly to my anxieties. I
suppose they've been exacerbated.
The lack of a goodbye, a hug, a backwards glance - the "I'm
sure we will meet again" -
It feels wretched.

Spoke in the Lyft to a man from Argentina about four months
with my girlfriend. He was marvelously consoling.

It is difficult to think that if I stayed in LA we could meet
again. Certainly this is all less your fault than I have woundedly made it out to be. It is by no fault of yours that I must
return home.

Part of me wants to say: you have been honest throughout,
gentle, maybe we are twins, I want to hear from you.

Part of me wants to say: you have taught me that maybe I am
not enough in myself.

And yet I can't leave it at that: hello, old friend

(I'm not sure what either of us could have done differently)

37. a gorgeously intelligent a heart-wrenching
and gentle and humane bridge across pain
you have effected, erected, made to materalize.
(I see I am condemned to repeat myself
In my appreciation of you.
The most original minds are also the fullest of repetition—
they grow proportionally,
like a boy.)
I only skimmed the email; was
reading university regulations online when the notification buzzed onto the top
of my screen—I read it darkly
almost before I saw your name.

I wondered if I would be able to read it
And then it blinded me with care
(I heard a businessman boast,
"I'll kill you with energy.")
And now my eyes fill with tears.

Tonight at dinner I told my mom I
didn't like the wine we were drinking
the Chianti
I felt like you, tasting, discerning,
instructing casually

I have always thought of myself as inconsistent,
particularly in tennis; have fetishized the opposite quality
in others; but right now I like myself
Inconsistent

I say that to begin to broach the subject.
I do like painting and you, religion.

And yet every truth-statement is true,
if controvertible
To explain thoroughly why I asked to
Watch Love Victor would be to
finish the work of philosophy.

I spoke to Baylor today, and to an Upper East Side psychiatrist I know, and they both said what I can glean on my walks, as facts revolve: that we are confused, young, that you do not despise me. I think our indecisiveness, a kind of pacifism, very beautiful. A kind of, well, quietism.

I feel held, healed, whole, writing this, perhaps because I have changed of late such that I cannot hear myself unless I am talking to, for, you.

we are sitting in a cul de sac together,
the one we always sit in, and you
are saying, "But don't we speak to
each other that way?"
And now you laugh at "She
feels a lot of pressure to be the
best Lucy she can be." Now
we walk on and the old woman
thanks us, for stepping aside,
but for doing so wrapped in each
others' arms

As always you have apprehended my
meaning better than I, detained it,
questioned it, set it free, benevolently.
You didn't misread me

Forgive my scattered response: you are
a street called ridgeview onto which I
have turned with Avatar trees and from this
ridge, this thin elevated lip of a path
curling upward from the dust
I have a pleasant view.

Strange, I have been musing that the lesson of the last four months (millennia?) is that I (one) oughtn't act on behalf of Ideals: yes, that they cripple action, blind us to what is before us: that we ought to use our finite time to take finite actions in order to relish finite delights, and that the ideal smothers us in infinity. SJWs seem to me smothered, deadened under ideals if also enlivened. Their true voices are muffled under some weak mesh of ideals. It is all related, naturally.

I am sure that to see things as they are is an incoherent ideal, the worst kind, or is that merely a redundancy? I agree that the lesson always slips away, that lessons are strictly not to be drawn from the story of Abraham, nor are ideals. Merely the story of a man. Certainly I would not ask for a sexless or verseless union. Probably I am just gesturing to my fear of those immensities.

"I only started watching tv a year ago"
(a noble sentence)
I feel I begin and end existences,
knowings, customs, every year, month,
day. But I find you unbeginnable
You fix me in place, put an axis in me
When did I begin to lavish praise?

Whence this affection

I suppose I love mirrored rules,
inheritances, gossip, folklore, scraps
of dialogue; I like to take every
suggestion as an awesome dictate;
like to pretend to be a written character
And tie myself to the mast of the law
of his destiny

Kellyanne says her family taught "self-denial"
The allure of this ideal is not easily
Vanquished in me

Transposed:
It was ours by being ours
That was how it was

Bad poetry, but I can live with that

38. Dear —,

I am not sure why I want so badly to hear from you but I do, and I can make some guesses, and some extrapolations.

Writing for myself has always been what soothed me, and this format is dangerously close to writing for myself; also, talking to you came to feel like talking to myself; so that I am inclined to say too much here.

Perhaps this is foolish of me, but I think I want to know the truth. I want to hear some account of what happened, if only because you were my witness for four months, four very long months, four very significant months—and I want to check my sense of reality against yours. Maybe you are protecting me—wisely, generously—but I'd feel saner if we had some frank discussion.

It seems probably not such a mystery to me—that there is such a thing as depression, and toward June with nothing to do I began to feel aimless and quasi-depressed; you felt this as my needing you, my not being able to walk beside you as an individual.

To say this is painful, and what I feared might happen after a season of buoyancy, and it also is probably not the only thing you began to notice about me (the way I talked to people, eg to your family) that you disliked—but it's something, something I can name, something I tried to warn you about but could not prepare you for—an explanation, at least.

Maybe you will know better than to tell me my shortcomings; you probably know best here, and I might as well thank you in advance.

It has been so long since you wrote in prose to me. Maybe it was only once or twice.

It is almost unbearably humid here!

39. I just remembered "subvert the prompt"

My mom keeps playing your music while she cooks

Down the street two Grand Cherokees, one white one black, on opposite sides of the street and facing different directions

GTI's everywhere these days

II.

40. I achieve a certain high from walking. I've resumed my walks across New York, though for now just over the Manhattan Bridge, into Chinatown, and back into Hasidic Williamsburg, over the Williamsburg. I didn't know quite how relieved, at ease, I would feel, being back here, and conversely how alienated and utterly oppressed by the house in Baltimore with my parents in it. The loops I walk make the city a map of my thoughts, a large subjective room. Everyone convinces me as I pass them—the beautiful rich women in simple expensive clothes biking back from their jobs in lower Manhattan, I imagine they have boyfriends, sororities, intense

drives, striking prejudices, inarticulate principles they've absorbed from their fathers... of course the Hasids, their coupledness, their sexlessness, the way the children play on scooters at the corner as though it's the fifties, the closed language, the closed text they study, the unreadable glances they shoot at me, the way they each do their duty—children sweeping, old women bargaining, young men fathering children... I suppose in their way the bums convince me, the Midwestern tourists with their bright colored, mall-fitted clothes convince me, the old poor Chinese women maybe not, but anyone on a bike, or a motorbike, or in a BMW or any car for that matter, they must have sacrificed, or lived, anyway they convince me—

I began to think: art can come later, or if it never comes is that such a loss. Obviously I am dangerously suggestible; susceptible to other people—but the charm of the lifestyle, the unabashed consumerism and overt fixation with money—with how much things cost, how much others are paying for other things—was considerable... there is a simplicity in that. Materially, it makes for an orgiastic life—Neronian, Athenian, whatever—and intellectually—well, who wants to worry about the intellectual lives of the people you live with?

41. Sitting down once more to reinvent the wheel for you, for me. It is a meditation, a discipline, a joy. I walked to Manhattan two hours ago and bought a French press, again. The last one I left with Cole. I wrote a long note after a walk the other night; it now feels dated. (My curse: to not believe my other moods, other selves.)

The last two weeks, looking back, are a maze. I have wandered, to little avail, except that my feelings have become more remote from me. I think we have already established that perspective is not something that can be achieved, not in the usual sense. Or, there is only muddled, human, time-bound perspective. To cut to the chase: I am wondering what has resurfaced, what has been tested by thought and now has the ring of truth. What have I determined, or learned? What we did was idealistic and beautiful. That is one thing. Little else beyond that is clear to me. Your point about our mutual indecisiveness—there was something to that. The time of your life, your having had it and my having had it—that sounds true too. I can see why history is hard to write. How are you?

42. Good morning. I opened Notes and this one just says, 'Like the strangers on a cruise perpetually bantering', which is from a lecture I watched by David Mamet from 2012 the other day, about becoming a conservative, and the rules that govern how we act in public, which he thinks say we must increasingly be polite, innocuous, shallow, that we are afraid of giving offense and so are prevented from saying meaningful things. Obviously a 2012 take and not a 2020 take. Anyway I thought it was an arresting image

Im writing and not speaking because everyone's in the apartment. Have no privacy

I didn't listen at four in the morning, but I did listen at seven, and then went back to sleep so that the memory of the nearly twenty minute message inevitably has the quality of a dream, cotton candyish, sweet and formless. It is funny this whole business of apologies, regret, negative and positive thinking - because no it did not and would not have ever seemed to me that you sounded snarky in the first message (though I like the thing of your having to explain that it was snarky), and more importantly, I am not upset with you, I am relieved and happy to be talking. Not only was the day-and-a-half silence not indicative of a general feeling, I don't think I would characterize even that as an instance of anger at you. I felt resigned or unwanted or maybe toyed with, but it was… well, I hate to say this, because so much of life is this way, and things with us should be non-this way, but… it was about me, I suppose. My aggression was directed toward myself, sadly.

I got a biography of proust that I think I'll read next. Do we both like biographies. This morning I lay in bed and listened to your message and smiled. I also looked at instagram for too long, bard people, I'm scared of images in a way, less than I used to be, there's no reason to be finally

While it seems obvious to me too that gossip can be gossip even if it's true i love that your dad takes the other position and think he's right to do so, it's in character, it has the truth of fiction

43. I like hearing you but find I don't enjoy leaving voice messages now, I'm uncomfortable doing so, maybe this is a passing thing

Using the Internet, listening to pop music, these are wrapped up in matters of shame, isolation, impatience, release. I resolved not to listen to Taylor Swift, why? Because I would like it? And then not know whether to tell you? and feel isolated, by having had another charged, secret experience—?

Knowledge, experience, emotion... they are a burden if they can't be shared. I like surfing the Internet more now, watching videos, knowing I can send them to you.

Had been thinking I was wrong about pop—what I said in the email was that it is outside my parents' small bandwidth, & that may be true, but truer, more to the point, is that it is a concentrated, even euphoric, at least heightened, experience... I have long thought that a great pop song is formally like a great poem or novel if only in that either can achieve formal perfection, a hermetic bliss, that in the case of pop is so recognizable, so briefly obvious and satisfying. Why I need such rich aesthetic experiences, is a question I won't think about now, but my parents are surely relevant.

The movie, Smiles of a Summer Night, is that what it's called? Such a childlike, such a translated, such an humanistic, such an inconsequential name, was such an unabashed masterpiece. R loves Bergman's memoir, says it's the best of its genre by far, and that his first three or so movies were technical catastrophes—out of focus or something—isn't that extraordinary? or ordinary? that the greatest people fail objectively?

I've been drinking the lowest quality coffee... watery, weak, tasteless, which I bought at Trader Joe's—Arabica, medium roast—seems wasteful to throw it out, and maybe this is a good opportunity for my tolerance to go down—the monk speaks.

44. Yet once more... (do you know this Milton poem, written when he was 24? a sort of elegy for his youth? Harry calls

it the finest short poem in the language, though it almost doesn't sound like English) I find myself feeling I need to sleep after a long day's work but feeling too that I must write you—as if I am an immigrant parent supporting a family, adhering to a schedule, cooking, disciplining the house—as if I have a job—and yet I've done barely anything today. I am wary of writing too baroque a letter—making too much of myself and my structureless weeks, my shameless freewheeling wasted time... I moved a rug, I wrote to my cousin about the news that she is expecting a baby, female, I browsed McNally Jackson, I watched Kamala's speech. What do you think of Kamala? She seems, finally, smart, decent, broadly conventional... like Joe. Donald is some kind of genius, animal, artist, freak, but I don't want an artist to helm the budget, the army, the newspaper leads.

I think of things to write you across the day, speculative letters coalesce and dissipate—I don't write them down. For a few years I carried a small notebook, so that I'd have a record of my thoughts. Later I decided that there is a subtler accretion in the mind, whereby traces of the truly memorable gather and swirl in the tides; writing partitions thoughts into droplets. I hardly have been writing or reading (my curse: to be monomaniacal).

I like the thought that everything is interchangeable—that a campaign speech is poetry, poems are politics, they're both a genre of sermon—that writing letters is a sort of job, that love is only as impersonal as the rest of life—which is all flux, all harsh, all strength, all subject to universal and unrelenting laws.

What do you make of this style? Would it have been different, typed? Would "it" have been "it"? Prose reverie let's call it. Yes, talking on the phone was a beautiful thing. A beautiful nothing (Harry would be proud of you).

Here I am, here we are, soldiering on through time, through space. Freer than anyone has ever been.

It is true, after all, that our age demands not only despair but exhilaration, at the thousand colors of the breaking glass, the phantasmagoria of total disarray. But here we are, talking about it. Friendship—an indestructible institution.

I have no idea where these words, this mood, came from. You can see, likely, why I never do anything—nobody would do anything if they perceived the connections, the interconnections among the world, as I did. Your email was vivid, interesting, narrative, suggestive—now I'm reading it a second time…—the portrait of Adam is amazing, I confess 'wandering curls' wounded me.

Ah, I can hear the tone you used with your mom, private, unyielding, ironic, with yourself for an audience… withholding from her, I mean.

(Elegance achieved against a mean & desperate face…)

I didn't know it was the 12th… 5th, 8th, 20th,
All big numbers and small, depending on your mood
Could it be that I'm losing count
Thank you for reminding me

I am proud of you, you are beautiful, I am sad you are far away, I couldn't see how miserable this job was for you, how taxing, I'm sorry, I love you

45. i've been watching videos of caitlin flanagan for an hour
before that was watching videos of abigail shrier, the beautiful jewess
went to columbia oxford and yale law school, lol, lives in los angeles
her parents were judges, her husband is a wealth manager whose office is a few blocks from your high school

caitlin flanagan is quite beautiful—was in a sorority at uva—i am fascinated. she speaks with the ease and assurance of someone who is not only very smart
but who has always succeeded, attracted the right kind of attention, is looked to physically with expectation, eagerness

somebody who has spent her whole life in the corridor of normativity, of playing the game, of illusion

this might seem pessimistic, or self-pitying, but it is also how i see my mom, and my dad

as never having been alienated. fascinatingly. to me

the difference between her and the other three women (dressed mournfully, politically, in black) is instructive and amazing

i don't mean to suggest that she isn't wonderful, doesn't think for herself in a gentle shrewd delightful way

46. Using a pen I got at the DMV—it has no logo on it—solid, chunky, blue—stylish—an accident? Sort of the way East Germany in the sixties is a style, inadvertently

I just walked down Franklin, which turns into Kent; Greenpoint quickly yields to Williamsburg then into impoverished Orthodox Williamsburg

The thrill for me, the rush, of black cousins with babies and balloons at a birthday party, a miles-wide sunset over the East River, finance guys with gelled hair, an Asian woman on a bike yelling at a fat girl who ambled into the bike lane "Come on white girl! Get with it!" is immense

Beautiful women are thrilling to me—the conditions of womanhood, of femininity are a great mystery, an undiscovered country

(You have just sent the text saying you are annoyed)

I don't think I caught, first time around, that you were saying it is a wish of mine that you not be gay—I don't think this is so much true as the fact of your seeming... in-between, an ambiguous case, in a way that makes you similar to me, similarly positioned. It makes me feel less alone, to know that there is someone like you (someone like me).

I do not wish that you or I were anyone else. Your words of an arresting email, earlier, come to mind: that the point is that things are as they are, that we have been 'given to' explore one difficult, exquisite corner of experience.

'Better (more true) to improvise, to be slow'

Do you still feel ill? Achey? Fevered? I of course would prefer that you are just being hypochondriacal

47. I am in bed now, naked. Evading, circling. The air conditioner lets out peculiar smells. We are always compromising ourselves in this life. We can never act quite fully consciously, but only by a kind of accident, or instinct.

Anyway, I am revolving what you said in my head. I couldn't focus today, was listening, looking up, scanning compulsively. I suppose because I have such expansive freedom, which can be paralyzing. Yet what a blessing, if I can be simple.

Thought on my walk about you and cooking—what your dad said—that you have spent years at it, have built on your experience, know so much. No grand conclusion, it just—impressed itself on me...

In a way, we are very simple. Too simple. Idealistic. Take people at their word. Want what is best. And so on.

If I am being honest: the debacle does not seem representative of general patterns. I was unusually irritable and sleep deprived, and the confusion across so many media was weird and unusual—

48. Edward and Cyrus just walked in, Edward was crashing, now is leaving to go and live with a sushi chef in New Haven and help him write a cookbook and film a cooking show. Be-

fore that was living on a farm in Louisiana with an old gay farmer. I am flustered, reddened as I looked up from typing to make small talk. The coffee I'm drinking seems burnt and ineffectual.

I've been thinking a bit about place—there is a system that says there are who people, where people, and what people. I would never have imagined myself to be a where person—a distant third. But the luminescence, the sense of new life, of the last four months seem to implicate the place. Or, I wonder what is possible here, what is replicable from the spring, what can be carried over (trans-fer, meta-phor) and new york seems a condemned place in my imagination, maybe only because it is too burdened with the past, my past.

Maybe it is worth asking again - how are you? Even to hear about tennis, a road trip, your wandering the backyard, meant something different and more to me than any speculation could.

i wrote katie a letter early on, late march perhaps, the one she didn't respond to, in which i said, I'd been thinking about "how form allows for differences… a poem allows you to say things that are otherwise very hard to say; the form of a romantic relationship allows you to express hopes and feelings it is hard to communicate elsewhere/otherwise." you helped me see that my language had been restricted, my risk aversion had been narrowing my life. by not saying certain words it had been impossible to imagine certain possibilities, enter certain states of mind.

49. That's also my thought about DFW committing suicide

It's remarkable how different you are from your mom
Except you're both matter-of-fact
Which I like
I (half an hour later:) wonder what would happen
if I asked to see you right now.
I won't; I'll take a walk (I...
Wonder how the family feels about Joey's
departure).
(a few hours later:) Oh God the smell of
The air and the insect-noises and the
empty backlit sky were so beautiful in the
park just now... I thought of all sorts of
things you'd said to me that I'd forgotten to
respond to... I'm sure I won't be able to
think of them now.

      A thought was that I could defer a year, we could go somewhere and work, make some money, I'm ambivalent about doing school remotely.

I wonder if you've written back yet. I feel I have to write before I check.

Walking is maybe the only time when I can hear myself
properly — walking alone or with you
I've come to think through my life while walking the
Way I used to think through what I'd say in a paper

That is to say: speak to myself, have visions, make
Arguments, wait for my own reaction
When I use apple products I seem not to be able
to detect that elusive voice that alone is generative
Only it can offer a positive vision
Only through it can I improvise

I've decided I agree: a month sounds perfect, give or take.
I will start looking
It will be memorable, dangerous, full, aesthetic
Delineated, sunny, romantic
(I love lists of adjectives)

Afterwards we could fly to New Hampshire if we wanted
My mom says the risk of contracting on the plane is low
She seems to have read up.

I think it is hard not to be impressed by status, achievement, money
But merely essential that we learn not to be
An essential common note, commonality, in
our childhoods must have been the discovery
of high culture—as an air, a realm, a possibility,
a reality, a multidirectional field that our parents
ignored, or seemed to have hid, in their single-minded
pursuit of visible success—the determined climb up a "ladder."

Nevertheless I wouldn't mind working some straightforward or straight-laced job in my twenties. In advertising or law or journalism—anything.

I think what I have recognized in you, had with you, is so new a category as to be a real problem for description. I mean, I would stay in LA... I don't think I can do better than to say the dream about sneaking through the house with the boy came true.

    At dinner they were talking as if LA were a small

town, which I liked. An industry town. Full of smart Jews...

50. Beep boop

7:57 where you are
Bon nuit where I am

I am home now but exhausted from last night
I don't want to give my thoughts short shrift
Want to give you a better missive tomorrow

Sounds like better kiss, masseuse, aperitif

Wonder what wonders this Sunday encapsuled for you
Like Capsule the startup, like a time capsule, like time
I miss our old resplendent emails
Not blaming or upset, just carried to a different moment

Much to say
I felt confident, canny, swaggering almost this evening
Pray for humility
There's some irony there

Good night

51. I have the impulse to reach into my head, pull out some of the thoughts that have been jangling

I just read a very very long piece in the times about breonna taylor - her life, her boyfriends, her city, the investigation that targeted her - I find myself liking what you said about the protests way back when - they seem like a part of god's plan - I am predictable, arent I

I looked up Andrew Sean Greer only after finishing the book - he is bumbling, faggy, a bit cringey - is married to a "management consultant in the tech industry" in san francisco, I don't know, I'm glad I read before researching - the medium matters, and the web videos and articles crushed him into something nervous, unappealing, conventional, scheming - whereas the novel was so gentle, stylish, light,

The bits of therapeutic talk you've given me over the last however long crop up in my head sometimes - life can only be lived forward, what if the point is that you have precisely the parents you have and not any others,

52. I'm tipsy, tired, the works. Only just seeing that the subject is "good morning"
recognizable, humorous, distinctive, human (these I think are basically synonyms)
I used to think about approximately that question: what was it like fifteen thousand years ago to know a language, or to meet a tribe that spoke a different language
Read books about native americans
kate gave me a book just now
that we'd gone to an event for, by its author, cyrus dunham, who amazingly has a name like cyrus duff, and is lena dunham's brother
and more memories (you are becoming my repository of memories, or... whatever), of: i couldn't sleep on a summer night in new haven, two years ago,
and picked up the collected stevens off the floor, read through

the... marginalia? notes? timelines? and finally essays
he accepted a prize once
and wrote, simply, humbly, stupidly, carefully, like a poet
you would like them! (the prose specimens)
i like them
He read widely, went to law school; is an example I contemplate every now and then
Funny, this: two nights ago, sleepless, I picked john ashbery up off the bedside table and read "litany"
a poem by a genius, a great poem, even though poems evaporate when they're not being read
dont have an effect, dont amount to anything - but while you're reading it - it is exciting, shall we say, and worth it

III.

53. I'm sitting in my attic, with a salad to my right, which I'm eyeing for my dessert.

I just talked to P on the phone, I won't tell you for how long, after biking back in the dark for the first time.

Had two glasses of wine while we talked. Complained of being in a stupor.

Today I got my computer back at the holy Apple Store, and so I can write an email to you during non-business hours. I saved your emails to my computer this afternoon, so I could look at them when I got back to the lair. This last week has been one of the highest-octane, whiplashiest, highest rate of new facts expectations customs circumstances adjusted to per hour, of my life.

It's felt weirdly normal. Or, Brooklyn and Buenos Aires and Los Feliz were expert preparation. This is easy by comparison. Ok, enough of that.

I didn't know Nietzsche had a book on representative men. Who are they? Have you read it? Emerson's unit, it occurred to me while thinking about your letters and mine, was the sentence. His essays can be read backwards or forwards. It's as if with each sentence he's starting over, starting a new life, a fresh attempt at being free and beautiful (and true). Your list of adjectives for Goethe, by the way, was very beautiful. Maybe it is accurate, too. Seems so. Bloom liked to refer to 'the tradition of European literature that went from Homer to Goethe', with that idea that he somehow contained everything that came before him. And yet: light-footed.

It makes me happy to hear you say you'd like to study art and teach painting—a huge and modest vision at once, delicate and expansive.

I don't know what the difference between critic and artist is. An artist seems like a bolder, rougher, more primitive, more ferocious version of the same thing. Borges has a thing about the difference between reading and writing. That reading is much more civilised, is the punchline. So I'm saying maybe: criticism is more civilised. I also happen to think it's the form suitable for our time, though that's hard to explain or defend.

I am not done, but:

warmly, affectionate, lovingly,

(I will obey my passing thoughts and record them: you helped me believe in high culture again, sort of, I think. R's parents were academics and so he rejects anything that reminds him of it. He is also straight and cynical and hates anything that seems sentimental or precious or pretentious or idealistic...

Strange for me to bring this up, since I am thinking of how relieved and refreshed I was to see the mention of Mendelssohn and Goethe, who he loves too, but I think it was the way you weaved them in: as part of a good life, things to be enjoyed without harsh irony and defensiveness.)

Here I am, spilling my mind to you as always. Our life together feels like a different universe. I think of July 4, 11 weeks ago, as the paradigmatic... moment, don't know why. Of the faraway time and place. It's funny—! It is so strange, the way I put down my thoughts unselfconsciously. And then I read you saying the same thing: "I don't have that impulse with you." To summarise, streamline, censor, shape, deform, elaborate, regurgitate, prove, etc.

Happy birthday to —. Tell him for me, if you would.

What was absurd about the Italian food?

Rhetoric ought to be taught: I and the Romans and Greeks and British agree with you.

You said many amazing and earnest and important things. I am excited, and have been thinking about the fact, that you applied to work as a cook at deep springs. Elliot who went to deep springs will come over for drinks with his girlfriend tomorrow - I think it is the girlfriend he told me about years ago when he grinded on me for half an hour at a party and I drunkenly asked him to come to my room, and he said, no, I have a girlfriend.

I feel it very strongly now in this cabin, this flat, this wooden dwelling high up in the trees with no internet. To go to bed with no option of going online is a wonderful anachronistic feeling. It reminds me (that feeling, and this house) of visiting my grandmother's farm house at 13 or 14, where there was nothing but old beautiful things, fields, hay, horses, gilt-bound books, cold air and ruddy people.

I share your nervousness, disgust, fatalism. Didn't watch the debate, but talked with P just now about his similar fears. Your sadness is more sane and mature than his fear. I suppose you know that you will be okay. And yet a dynasty, or a long slow descent, into a stalled economy and open corruption and one-party control or some picture like that, is depressing. I wonder though, how much did you or I ever care about America? It seems we knew better than to make liberalism central to our identity. Right? Weren't we onto something? I'm not making a joke. There are more enduring things. Transcendental beauty, eg.

My old joke (a few months old): MacBook Air prose. Whereas your emails were weighed, weighted, considered, sculpted. In any case - for my last trick -

I think I'm going to memorise the poem now. Good night. I miss our nightly calls. Maybe one of these early mornings, if you are up at 11 or 12, I'll send an invitation.

60. Good morning. Typing on flip phone. Thank god for fresh air. Congratulations on your book, an amazing feat. Strangely I also struggled with the news somehow. No one likes the video, including me, but it seems like the only way to get an

agent in this day and age. I have been feeling not good. Too much to update you on right here, right now. Thanks for writing back...

54. Pasta again, wine again, nighttime again.
I'm looking over your earlier letter and it's stimulating me.

Your vision of America is whimsical and idealistic and beautiful — I think right, in that Whitman couldn't have flowered anywhere else.

My eye wanders down the page — Leo Strauss — yesterday I read the Straussian Moment, a weird impressive "essay" by Peter Thiel — billionaire, gay, Libertarian.

One finds one's community without too much trouble — one's "clime," one's friends.

There is lots of violence in America—lots of hunger—I don't think these are its strong points—I think its strong point is some kind of guilelessness, simplicity, childishness, freedom.

One way to summarize what I've concluded in the last two years is that I don't believe in generalizations—I believe in spontaneity, I believe in personality, energy, violence—in being strong enough to speak with "isaac" at any given moment. In a way, I went here to counteract that—to crush or suppress the Emersonian in me, the antichrist. But I haven't repented yet.

One feels the more one says, the more one has to say, no? Which favors whoever starts earliest and goes hardest.

Which is unfair, but exquisite...

Fear and longing

A special club

I keep dreaming that I am with my middle school friends Matthew and Daniel at a bar mitzvah, or with my camp friends on a bus, then waking up alone in England, like I'm 12 again, in my parents' house...

I think people like us feel this way—outside the circle—and seek out clubs... the Thomas Aquinas scholar has studied and taught at Yale, Harvard, Oxford and Cambridge which seems... corny, transparent.

Feel I must apologize for staying quiet for so long after such a revealing, such an epic, letter. I'm sorry about CJ, ... I don't know what it's like, and don't want to, I hope you never have to know that pain or fear or confusion again. It is dark and awful to think of her liking your pictures on Facebook.

I guess you know I've banished the computer from my "flat" and so I won't send this or see if you've responded to yesterday's letter for about 18 hours, starting now... my therapist used the word "invalidation" the other day. I wonder if CJ felt "invalidated."

I think there is a great goodness here too.

I read more psalms this morning: "my days are like a shadow that declineth."

To be inspired by the title alone—that seems the whole point—of style, art, love; for everything to be suffused with beauty and inspiration.

55. The gas fireplace is going, water is on to boil, clothes are in the drier tumbling, and on my bed too, warm ready to be folded. Dishes piled in the sink, parmesan cheese grated, red wine in a glass in front of me, as well as your "writings." A pen in my hand. The machinery of life is going. I have not been feeling very good.

I wrote a long email last week about what I'd done in the last year, the impetus being my self-chastisement: 'you've done nothing in the last year'. I didn't send to you because you featured in it, but I should, will.

The people here are simply very smart, mature, serious, knowledgable. It is funny to guess for so long what people will be like then be confronted with speaking, Zooming people. I've seen the legendary creatures with my own eyes (on videochat).

It is deeply comforting to live on the third floor of an old married couple's house. I am their child and this is my house. Today I thought about the poem you'd sent me & felt grateful.

Have we met somewhere before? I remember you dimly.

Every Adam belonging to me, as good belongs to you…

A remarkable way to end a book—yes.

I have never felt more like a wandering Jew. Not in Argentina or New York. Maybe because I am older. Yet I feel at home. In England, in school, in this house. I have a nice new advisor of sorts – Daniel Weiss – American, jew, writes on ancient scripture and modern Jewish philosophy (Benjamin, Rosenzweig).

I feel very empty and very full. It is a rich experience to hear from you and yet I feel wounded in the recognition of your voice.

56. It is good to get your efflux
your outflowing

to catch it

i just realized i have done no 'work'
in the two months that i have been here.
feels like more like six.

yes - edward not long ago was looking into buying a cheap house, i think in vermont. may have corresponded with some real estate agents. made me aware of the potential there

i just took a moment to look at farms in france where i could go live and work. maybe ill do that next year and finally learn french.

i'm friends with an italian classicist/hebraist who offered to meet once a week and teach me greek. it all sounds a little too ideal. we'll see what comes of it.

yes to live in the mountains or country... probably would be best? i used to think i wanted to live in the biggest city, or failing that at a school filled with young people. but now im learning that i want neither. a town or village would be plenty of people for me. where i live now is near a field where sometimes at 3:45 in the afternoon the sky lights up pink and orange and purple. i see foxes, fields with hedges around them, signs in the middle of fields that inexplicably say 'deep water' or 'private property'.

roger staggers around the house looking for his wife, saying "darling? darling" in his very proper accent. they are both so attractive and healthy and appealing, don't seem to realize they're in their seventies, or dont care. he cooks astounding meals every night for her, yesterday surprised me with lunch: duck with seared potatoes and pearl onions and carrots, and she maid some kind of apple crumble with fresh cream on top. afterwards i felt horrible, i'm not used to such richness

57. Hello

I know it is too early for me to ask for your forgiveness

(I hope you're good)

Just had someone say ugly things to me because I didn't reciprocate his interest in dating

Life is very short, very long, very brutal, very precious

The day before I texted you I watched a video about how to

tie a noose

I'm slowly learning to live with my moods

58. i'm feeling as bad as i've ever felt, which is… well, saying something
to which what can one say? except: sorry to hear that

i still don't know how to interpret "i'd like to"
you probably dont realize that its phrased in almost the most noncommittal way possible
i don't think it's intentional, but it is, i'm afraid, typical
tell me if i seem to be wrong

i haven't gone to any classes this term, or written the paper i was supposed to

why is the rich lunch making you laugh?
because of my inept description?
or the food itself?
or that i couldnt stomach it?

as always, i wonder why you are telling me these things
the man who knew too much is a good title, isnt it
like ecclesiastes

i enjoyed talking to you, pretty recently

i don't know what to say
i'm not well

59. It sucks that we are perpetually misunderstanding each other. Obviously. After my note about Northrop Frye and my mother and great grandmother and myself etc, I was expecting some response in kind. I had had such a nice time talking a few days before that. (I do not feel I have someone I can speak with freely and regularly.) I interpreted your sarcastic one-line "This is uncanny" email as some kind of blunt dismissal. (I was particularly self-conscious about the reference to the writer who traveled on an inheritance; thought it might be distasteful or worse.) I think I waited a few more days and then was very upset, that you seemed to have broken off... what seemed a friendly exchange. Goodbye was a rash word sent from my phone. Best wishes was the automatic signature that I forgot would show up.

I turned to Northrop Frye out of sadness and frustration, with my work here. I wrote about him (and Jeremiah and Roger and Melania) to you out of the same spirit. I wrote the "travelogue" quickly out of the same spirit again. I wonder why you couldn't read on. I wonder why not one person, not even my parents, responded to the travel email. The smallest acknowledgement is helpful. I know I'm often cryptic as a result of my reluctance to ask for what I want directly. But in the name of being straightforward: I would be happy to hear from you. I know in October and November you were quite open; there were long emails about skiing; and I wasn't so responsive. But the conversation a few weeks ago was pleasant and I thought it would be possible to continue in that vein.

60. Enjoyed roving over the conversation in my head this morning.

61. (A year later)
It is time—
not to be alone with oneself again. To have the regular intercourse.

We share, I should think, a sense of lateness, a sense of the moment's having come and gone and living in the cold wake, the extending shadow.

Why don't I talk to you directly: I want this as much as you. I concluded with someone a few years ago that one's life is over around 20, or that ours were anyway, and all that remains is to reproduce your life, in the form of children or writing. A backwards glance.

Yesterday I saw Cries and Whispers (I'd considered asking you to that instead). The joke is that everyone wants to kill themselves in it except the sister who is dying. But it doesn't matter that she is dying and is in pain. She is generous and unpretentious and pious in her way.

I think if I could learn to be more expressive in conversation it wouldn't have to pour out in sentences that sound like this. I have undergone so much pain in the last few years. Everyone walks around with such pain and moments of self-disclosure like this might enhance pain but they also relieve it temporarily.

I have never read Louise's poems except one or two which were middling. I have to thank you for your Soonest Mended email—I have fallen in love with Ashbery and have been reading widely in it.

I forgot to eat lunch today.

I've been thinking for a year now that one day I would send you a text out of the blue saying "I was thinking we should get married." You would just have to promise me 2-3 kids and that I would never have to set foot in Brooklyn again.

You looked wonderful today.

I can't send this of course, not right now.

Nachleben
Copyright © 2022 Nachleben
& Respective Authors

nachleben.biz

www.ingramcontent.com/pod-product-compliance
Lightning Source LLC
Chambersburg PA
CBHW051700040426
42446CB00009B/1228